Contents

The
Underground

Brandon Robshaw

Published in association with
The Basic Skills Agency

Hodder & Stoughton

A MEMBER OF THE HODDER HEADLINE GROUP

Acknowledgements
Illustrations: Alan Jackson
Cover: Getty Images/Photodisc

Orders: please contact Bookpoint Ltd, 130 Milton Park, Abingdon, Oxon OX14
4SB. Telephone: (44) 01235 827720, Fax: (44) 01235 400454. Lines are open from
9.00–6.00, Monday to Saturday, with a 24 hour message answering service.

British Library Cataloguing in Publication Data
A catalogue record for this title is available from The British Library

ISBN 0 340 86938 0

First published 2001
This edition published 2002
Impression number 10 9 8 7 6 5 4 3 2 1
Year   2007 2006 2005 2004 2003 2002

Typeset by SX Composing DTP, Rayleigh, Essex.
Printed in Great Britain for Hodder & Stoughton Educational, a division of
Hodder Headline Plc, 338 Euston Road, London NW1 3BH by Athenaeum
Press, Gateshead, Tyne and Wear.

1

Late for Work

Penny was late for work.
Again.
For the third time that week.
Her boss would kill her.

She ran to the tube station.
It was a cold, grey, rainy day.
There weren't many people about.
She showed her tube pass to the guard.
She ran down the escalator.
The station was empty.
She must be very late indeed.
She was so late she'd missed the rush hour!

It was a bit funny, though.
You'd expect a few people to be still around.
She looked at her watch.
Twenty to ten.
She looked at the indicator board.
Three minutes to the next train.
The destination was blank.
That was a bit funny, too.

She walked up and down the platform.
Her footsteps echoed
in the empty station.
She wished she was at home.
Tucked up in her nice warm bed.

There was a rushing noise.
The train was coming.

The doors opened. Penny jumped on.

2

'Now We're All Here'

The carriage was very full.
That was funny, thought Penny.
The station had been empty.
But the train was packed.

Everyone was looking at Penny.
She looked down at the floor.
She hated being stared at.

She hadn't really looked at the people.
But she got the feeling that they were
all very ugly.
Very, very ugly.
Maybe that was because
she was in a bad mood.

There was one empty seat.
Penny sat down in it.
She opened her newspaper.
She held it up in front of her face.

The doors closed.
The train moved off.

Then a thin, high voice said,
'Now we're all here.'

3

A Tap on the Arm

A chill ran through Penny.
What did that mean,
'Now we're all here'?

She didn't look up.
She knew they were all looking at her.
She stared at her newspaper.
She wasn't taking in the words, though.
There was something funny about this train.
She wished she'd stayed at home in bed.
Phoned in sick.

Then Penny felt a tap on her arm.
She jumped.

'Excuse me.'
It was the same thin, high voice as before.
It came from the man sitting next to her.

Penny put down her newspaper.
She looked around.
Then she screamed.

4
Boris

The man was very, very thin.
His skin was yellow.
His eyes were sunken.
He was totally bald.
He had no teeth.
He looked like a dead man.
He smelt like one, too.

Penny had never seen
such a horrible face.
She realised she was trembling.

Penny pulled herself together.
Stop it, she told herself.
The poor man must be ill.
He can't help the way he looks.
Or smells.

'Yes?' she said.
She tried to smile.
'What is it?'

'I thought I'd say hello.
We're going to spend a long time together.
I'm Boris.'

He put out his hand.
Penny shook it.
It was as cold as a toad.
'I'm Penny.
But I don't think
we'll spend much time together.
I'm only going five stops.'

Everyone laughed at this.
Penny felt uneasy.
Why were they laughing?
And why hadn't they stopped yet?
She looked at her watch.
Ten minutes had gone by.
Yet they still hadn't gone through a station.

'Excuse me?' she asked Boris.
'Is this the Bank train?'

Everyone laughed again.
'You've got a good sense of humour,'
said Boris.

The woman next to her
tapped her on the arm.
'What did you die of, dear?'

5

'You're All Dead!'

Penny looked round.

The woman's face was grey.
A sort of bluish grey.
Her eyes were bloodshot.
She didn't look at all well.
'I'm Suzi,' she said.
'I took an overdose.
It was a cry for help.
But no-one came to help me.'

'It was poisoning in my case,' said Boris.

'What about you?' asked Suzi.
'What did you die of?'

Penny looked round the carriage.
No-one looked normal.
Everyone had something wrong with them.
Some people looked very, very old and ill.
Some were as thin as skeletons.

'You – you're all dead!' said Penny.

'That's right, dear,' said Suzi.
'Just like you.'

'But – but I'm not dead!' said Penny.

'Yes you are,' said Boris.
'You must be.
We're all dead.
They said we had to go to Hell.
They put us on this train.'

'Who did?'

'The Authorities,' said Boris.
He shuddered.
'Let's not talk about them.'

'But – I shouldn't be here!' said Penny.
This was like a bad dream.
'I'm not dead!
I shouldn't be here!'

'Maybe there's been a mix-up,' said Suzi.

'That's right, there has!' said Penny.
'There's been a mix-up.
I'll tell them at the other end.
They'll have to let me go!
Send me back!'

'I bet they don't,' said Boris.

6
Next Stop: Hell

It started to get colder.
The train drew into a station.
It had dark grey walls.
Signs in red said 'Hell'.

The doors opened.
'Come on, dear,' said Suzi.
She took Penny by the arm.

The crowd of dead people
shuffled along the platform.
Some could hardly walk.

It got colder and colder.
Penny was shivering now.
Her heart was thumping in her chest.

At the end was a sign saying 'Way In'.
A man stood there,
counting off the dead people as they went by.
He had a clipboard in his hand.
He wore a uniform.
He had a small moustache
and small, sharp eyes.

Penny stopped in front of him.
'Excuse me,' she said.
Her voice was shaking.
'There's been a mix-up.
I'm not dead.'

'Just go through, please,' said the man.
Penny couldn't see what was through the door
behind him.

It was just a black triangle.
She could feel a draught
of freezing air coming from it.
There was a cold, metallic smell,
like hospitals.

'Go on,' said the man sharply.
'Don't hang about.
Get in there.'

'You tell him, dear,' said Suzi.

'There's been a mix-up.
I'm not dead!
Look, my heart is still beating!
You should send me back!'

'I don't want no trouble,' said the man.
'Just you go through,
or it'll be the worse for you.'

'But I'm not dead!' said Penny.
'Look, I bet my name's not on your list.'
The crowd behind was pushing her forward.
She had to struggle to stay where she was.

'You're causing a hold-up!'
said the man angrily.
'If you won't go through,
I'll have to call the Supervisor.'

'Call him, then,' said Penny.

'Right,' said the man. 'I will.
You asked for this.'

He took out a whistle and blew it.

7
The Supervisor

The Supervisor was a huge, fat, pale man.
He had a thin, cruel mouth,
like a line drawn across his face.
He was wearing a white suit.
The air seemed to get even colder
when he arrived.

'What's the problem here?' he asked.

'We've got a trouble-maker here,'
said the man with the clipboard.

The Supervisor looked at Penny.
He narrowed his eyes.
'A trouble-maker, eh?
Well, we know how to deal with those,
don't we?'
He laughed.
So did the man with the clipboard.

'I'm not a trouble-maker!' said Penny.
'But I shouldn't be here!
I'm not dead!
Look – check your list.
My name won't be there.'

The Supervisor took the clipboard.

'What's your name?'

'Penny Gibson,' said Penny.
'And I'm not on the list, am I?'

The Supervisor looked at the list.
Then he sighed.
'You're right,' he said grumpily.
'Those idiots!
Can't they get anything right?
We can't let you in here
if you're not dead.
It's against the rules.'

'That's right!' said Suzi.
'So you'll have to let her go.'

A feeling of relief swept over Penny.
She felt weak at the knees.
She was going to be free!

8
Fixing the Problem

'What are we going to do?'
asked the man in uniform.
He looked at Penny with dislike.
'We're not going to let this trouble-maker go,
are we?'

The Supervisor scratched his head.
'I don't want to let her go,' he said slowly.
'But how can we let her in?
I could get into trouble over this.'

'There must be something we can do,'
said the man in uniform.

'I don't know . . .' said the Supervisor.

'You'll have to let me go!' said Penny.
'You said it yourself.
You can only let dead people in.
I'm not dead.
So you'll have to let me go.'

'It is a problem,' said the Supervisor slowly.
Then his fat face brightened.
He smiled a thin smile.
'But I think we can fix it.'

He put his huge, fat, pale hands
around Penny's throat.
'Yes, I think we can fix it,'
he said again, as he began to squeeze.

9
Late for Work Again

Penny screamed.
She opened her eyes.
She sat up in bed.
She could still feel the fat man's hands
around her throat.
What a terrible dream!

She looked at the clock.
Oh, no!
It was quarter past nine.

She jumped out of bed
and got dressed.
She was late for work.
Again.
For the third time that week.
Her boss would kill her.

She ran to the tube station.
It was a cold, grey, rainy day.
There weren't many people about.

She showed her tube pass to the guard.
She ran down the escalator.
The station was empty.
That was a bit funny.
She looked at the indicator board.
Three minutes to the next train.
The destination was blank, though.
That was a bit funny, too.
Penny had a funny feeling
that this had all happened before.

Or she'd had a dream like this.
She couldn't remember it now, though.
Funny . . .

She heard the sound of the train coming.
The sound frightened her.
She didn't know why.